"The greatest obstacle to discovery is not ignorance,
it is the illusion of knowledge."
~Daniel J. Boorstin

D1468805

How To Stay
Motivated
During Difficult Times

Open this book in any page and find
Relevant
Answers to your current challenges

by Andres Lara
Professional Speaker

Library of Congress Control Number: 2003098370
ISBN: 0-9725166-1-1

Copy right 2004
by
By TheCubanGuy.com

How should this book be read?

This book should be read in no particular order. Just open it in any page and read the two pages facing you. On the left page, you will find my life-altering, insightful inspirations. On the right page you will find an inspirational story, a set of quotes or poem that to an extent parallels my message.

The stories, quotes, and poems on the right are some of the most inspiring pieces that top motivational speakers from all around the world use to touch, move, and inspire their audiences. These are the stories and quotes that have inspired me throughout my journey. I am certain that they will inspire you as well.

Though the principles in this book are simple, they are often neglected and not put into use. Remember, **lots of people know what to do, but only a few people do what they know.** My challenge to you is to use this book as a reminder. Whenever you feel challenged by life, just pick up this book, open it in any page, and read those two pages.

This book is not for everyone. It was written only for those who are in the constant pursuit of the best life has to offer. These are the people, who like me, encounter more rejection, more opposition, more challenges than the average person who accepts whatever life hands to them. This book is designed to encourage those people to take another step, to keep moving forward, to refuse to settle, and to gain a different perspective on what's currently happening.

Executive Editor: Rosa Carusone
Chief Editor: Josephine Carusone

How To Stay Motivated During Difficult Times

1

Step Up

Each rung in a ladder can support you, long enough, until you are able to give the next step up. Stand eternally on any particular rung, and it will eventually collapse.

Life is a ladder of many rungs. Don't get too comfortable, wherever you are or wherever you stand. Keep stepping up.

Step up towards the summit of that which you once intended to step up to. Step up towards that which calls you, excites you, intimidates you. What's the next step up your ladder? Step up before it's too late.

"The rung of a ladder was never meant to rest upon, but only to hold your foot long enough to enable you to put the other one somewhat higher."   *~T. H. Huxley*

Ladder of Achievement

"If you wish to know the mind of other people, listen to their words."
~Chinese Proverb

___100 % I did
___ 90% I will
___ 80% I can
___ 70% I think I can
___60% I might
___ 50% I think I might
___ 40% What is it?
___ 30% I wish I could
___ 20% I don't know how
___10% I can't
0% I won't

Author Unknown
Source: Ambassador of Excellence

"Beware of your words for they tell the world about your attitude. Beware of your attitude for it foretells the world about your future and about how far you'll get." ~Andres Lara

"Attitude is the speaker of your present and the prophet of your future." ~J.C. Maxwell

"Nothing can ever stop you if you have the right mental attitude; nothing on earth can help you if you have the wrong mental attitude." ~Thomas Jefferson

Start Living

2

Everything in life must have a beginning, as well an ending. As much as you resist it, everything was created with an end in mind, including you.

As Evan Esar once said, 'You can't do anything about the length of your life, but you can do something about its width and depth.' Dying should not be the worst of your fears; not having lived should be your worst fear. Start living.

What is the one thing that, if you did, would add more meaning to your existence and more depth to your life? Start living. Do it today.

"Live as you would have wished to live when you come to die."
~*Gellert*

Make Your Move

As you're reading this, your life
Is getting shorter, is fading
Is ticking away

I'm not saying this to frighten you
Or even to scare you
Though it may

I'm saying this, because I care
I'm saying this to resuscitate you from your deep slumber
I'm saying this to prepare you

Because you won't live forever
Because you shouldn't merely subsist
Because you were born for much, much, more

You were born to succeed
You were born to share your unique gifts
You were born to shine, brightly shine

Remember, the clock is ticking
The world needs you
Make your move; it's later than you think

Author: ~Mike Litman, http://www.mikelitman.com
Co-author #1 Best-Selling book Conversations with Millionaires

"Death is not the greatest loss in life. The greatest loss is what dies
inside us while we live."
~Norman Cousins

Trust Your Inner Wisdom

3

Do you know how to make your heart beat, your blood circulate, or your stomach digest?

Regardless of your not knowing, all of those functions and many others do get done continuously. They are delegated to and handled by your inner wisdom.

Trust your inner wisdom. Today, attempt something whether you know how to do it or not.

"You may be deceived if you trust too much, but you will live in torment if you don't trust enough."   *~ Frank Crane*

Thrive On Miracles

You don't need an explanation for everything. Recognize that there are such things as miracles, events for which there are no explanations. Later, knowledge may explain those events quite easily.

Yet for now, believe that for which you have sufficient evidence, and suspend your judgement when you have none. Some things have to be believed to be seen. And some things don't need to be seen to be believed.

Source: Inspiration University

"For those who believe, no miracle is necessary. For those who doubt, no miracle is sufficient."
~Nancy Gibbs

"Seeing, hearing, feeling, are miracles, and each part and tag of me is a miracle."
~Walt Whitman

"To get the tangible things that you desire, you must first trust in the intangible things that you fear."
~Andres Lara

4

Make A Move

You can be in the right place, at the right time, and around the right people; yet nothing will happen unless YOU make the right move.

Your first move won't necessarily be the best move, yet you will never make the best move unless you are willing to put up with the risk of making few poor ones.

Remember that anything worth doing well is worth doing poorly at first. The right move of tomorrow will evolve from your poor moves of today. Make a move and let it evolve.

"Excellence can be achieved, but first you must be willing to look foolish and make mistakes." *~Andres Lara*

Anyway

People are often unreasonable, illogical, and self-centered; Forgive them anyway.

If you are kind, people may accuse you of selfish, ulterior motives; Be kind anyway.

If you are successful, you will win some false friends and some true enemies; Succeed anyway.

If you are honest and frank, people may cheat you; Be honest and frank anyway.

What you spend years building, someone could destroy overnight; Build anyway.

If you find serenity and happiness, they may be jealous; Be happy anyway.

The good you do today, people will often forget tomorrow; Do good anyway.

Give the world the best you have, and it may never be enough; Give the world the best you've got anyway.

You see, in the final analysis, it is between you and God; It was never between you and them anyway.

~Mother Teresa

message

5

Uncertainty

Dare to take an action today whether you are certain about its outcome or not. Why?

Imagine you are in a foreign city. With only fifty dollars in your pocket, you jump into a taxi and ask the driver not to drive until you are certain about where you should go. An hour later, haven't moved an inch, the meter marks fifty dollars.

Don't forget that the meter of life is like that of a taxi; it will keep on ticking whether you are getting somewhere or just standing still.

"Being certain, knowing the ending of things before the beginning, causes much unhappiness; for it puts a knife in the heart of wonder."
~Tad Williams

The Road To Success

There is a curve called failure,
A loop called confusion,
Speed bumps called friends,
Red lights called enemies,
Caution lights called family.
You will have flats called jobs, but
If you have a spare called determination,
An engine called perseverance,
Insurance called faith,
A driver called desire,
You will make it to a place called success!
~Author Unknown

"The road to success is always under construction."
~Unknown

"The first step toward success is taken when you refuse to be a captive of the environment in which you first find yourself daily."
~Mark Caine

"Remember, we become who we spend time with. The quality of a person's life is most often a direct reflection of the expectations of their peer group. Choose your friends well."
~Anthony Robbins

"There's no secret about success. Did you ever know a successful person who didn't tell you about it?"
~Kin Hubbard

message

6

Reluctance

The easy becomes difficult when it's done with reluctance; the difficult becomes impossible when it's done with cynicism.

Add ease to your life. If you are to do something, do it whole-heartedly as though your enthusiasm will be the determining factor in whether it can happen or not.

Remember, battles are won not in the battlefield, but the night before when soldiers made up their minds that victory was guaranteed. Approach every task today as if its success is assured and victory will follow.

"There is nothing so easy but that it becomes difficult when you do it reluctantly."   *~Publius Terentius Afer*

The Two Wolves

An elder Cherokee native American was teaching his grandchildren about life. He said to them, "A fight is going on inside me... it is a terrible fight and it is between two wolves."

"One wolf represents fear, anger, envy, sorrow, regret, greed, arrogance, self-pity, guilt, resentment, inferiority, lies, false pride, superiority, and ego. The other stands for joy, peace, love, hope, sharing, serenity, humility, kindness, benevolence, friendship, empathy, generosity, truth, compassion, and faith."

"This same fight is going on inside you, and inside every other person too." The grandchildren thought about it for a minute and then one child asked his grandfather, "Which wolf will win, grandfather?" The old Cherokee replied, "The one you feed."
~Author Unknown

"Our doubts are traitors and make us lose the good we might win, by fearing to attempt."
~William Shakespeare

"You become what you think about most of the time."
~~Earl Nightingale

7

Give It Time

There's always something good behind every failure, there is always an opportunity behind every accident, there's always a gain behind every loss.

There is profit to be made out of your current difficulties. Not necessarily monetary, but a far more valuable profit. A profit that will never bankrupt on you. Spiritual and emotional profit.

The heavier the burden, the stronger you'll become. Give it time and remember that every cloud has a silver lining.

"Life's challenges are not supposed to paralyze you, they're supposed to help you discover who you are."

~*Bernice Johnson Reagon*

Success Trivia

1-Who ran for public office seven times, was defeated every time, and still went on to become president?
Abraham Lincoln

2-Who struggled through thousands of experiments before perfecting one invention and was rewarded over one thousand patents for his inventions?
Thomas Edison

3-Who didn't learn to talk until he was four years old and was told "he would never amount to anything", yet became the greatest thinker of our generation?
Albert Einstein

4-Who was told at an early age that he had no talent for music but whose name is synonymous with music quality?
Ludwig van Beethoven

5-Who was dismissed from the psychiatric society in Vienna, Austria, only to become a world respected, prominent psychiatrist?
Victor Frankl

~Author Unknown
Submitted by: Bonnie

"Both tears and sweat are salty, but they render a different result. Tears will get you sympathy, sweat will get you results."
~Jesse Jackson

8

Ask For It

If one out of the four wheels in your car made a squeaky noise, what wheel would you put grease on?

The squeaky wheel always gets priority over the other ones, if not all the grease. Wheels ask for what they need by squealing; without the squeal, you will never know of their need for grease.

The wheel squeals, a baby cries, you might simply have to ask. What are some of the things that you yearn for? More love? More recognition? More intimacy? Squeal for it by simply asking.

"You create your opportunities by asking for them."

~Patty Hansen

Asking: Quotes

"What I point out to people is that it's silly to be afraid that you're not going to get what you want if you ask. Because you are already not getting what you want. Without asking you already have failed, you already have nothing. What are you afraid of? You're afraid of getting what you already have! Who cares if you don't get it when you ask for it, because, before you ask for it, you don't have it anyway. So there's really nothing to be afraid of."
~Marcia Martin

"Great things are only possible with outrageous requests"
~Thea Alexander

"Ask, and it shall be given you; seek; and you shall find; knock and it shall be opened unto you. For every one that asketh receiveth; and he that seeketh findeth; and to him that knocketh it shall be opened."
~Bible (Matthew 7:7-8)

"You don't always get what you ask for, but you never get what you don't ask for... unless it's contagious!"
~ Franklyn Broude

"Others have seen what is and asked why. I have seen what could be and asked why not."   *~ Robert F. Kennedy*

"Ask and you'll be a fool for five minutes, don't ask you'll be a fool forever" *~Chinese Proverb*

One Thing To Fear

9

There is only one thing you should fear and that's to experience no fear.

Fear is experienced when you challenge the unchallenged, when you question the unquestioned, when you move beyond that point where your confidence drops, your doubts rise, and your certainty melts.

Just like giving birth to a quadruple; the birth of fear is a signal. A signal that, its siblings, growth, innovation, and progress are on the way.

"Having an abortion to kill fear, will not only kill fear but also its siblings— growth, innovation, and progress."

~Andres Lara

IF

If you can keep your head when all about you
Are losing theirs and blaming it on you;
If you can trust yourself when everyone doubts you,
But make allowance for their doubting too;
If you can wait and not be tired by waiting,

If you can dream--and not make dreams your master;
If you can think--and make thoughts your aim;
If you can meet with triumph and disaster
And treat those two impostors just the same;
If you can bear to hear the truth you've spoken twisted
Or watch the things you gave your life to break,
And build them up again;

If you can make one heap of all your winning
And risk it on one turn of pitch-and-toss,
And lose, and start again at your beginnings
And never breathe a word about your loss;

If you can talk with crowds and keep your virtue,
Or walk with kings--nor lose the common touch;
If neither foes no loving friends can hurt you;
If you can fill the unforgiving minute
With sixty seconds' worth of distance run--
Yours is the Earth and everything that's in it,
~Rudyard Kipling

"If you find a path with no obstacles, it probably doesn't lead anywhere."
~Unknown

10

Give It A Try

You can either control your fears or allow your fears to control you.

Long ago, a simulation of a real person was created to keep crows from eating the harvest. Crows feared this human simulation as much as they feared real people. The simulation was named scarecrows.

How do you know what's real and what's not? How do you know that what you fear at this moment is not but a harmless simulation? There is only one way to find out. Give it a try.

"Fear defeats more people than any other one thing in the world."
~*Ralph Waldo Emerson*

Fear: Quotes

"Live by what you trust, not by what you fear."
~Unknown

"No matter how hard you work for success if your thought is saturated with the fear of failure, it will kill your efforts, neutralize your endeavors and make success impossible."
~Baudjuin

"If you want to conquer fear, don't sit home and think about it. Go out and get busy."
~Dale Carnegie

"If you know no fear, you can fear not. If you know no failure, you can fail not. If you know no doubt, you can doubt not."
~Anonymous

"Never let the fear of striking out get in your way."
~Babe Ruth

Being Exposed

11

Beware of your actions, for they reveal how you truly feel about the people and things around you.

If there was someone who will expose your most guarded thoughts to the world, would you be concerned about this person? Well, such person does exist. You are it. You expose yourself through your actions.

Your mouth can lie, but your actions cannot. Likewise, to figure out how others feel about a cause, simply take a close look at their actions towards it. Remember, your actions speak so loud that others cannot hear what you are trying to say.

"The actions of men/women are the best interpreters of their thoughts."
                                                              ~John Locke

Human Relations' Course

The six most important words:
I admit that I was wrong.
The five most important words:
You did a great job.
The four most important words:
What do you think?
The three most important words:
Could you please. . .
The two most important words:
Thank you.
The most important word:
We.
The least important word:
I.
~Author Unknown

"You are the sum of your actions, of what you have done, of what you can do, Nothing else."
~Mahatma Gandhi

"The reason there are so few good talkers in public is that there are so few thinkers in private."
~ Source Unknown

"Get someone else to blow your horn and the sound will carry twice as far." *~Will Rogers*

Another Try

12

There are many battles you must fight to get to the top. You might not win all of them. Do not get discouraged!

Success means winning the war not every battle. Some battles will be lost, others will be won; some battles will be painful, others will be painless.

Remember, you win some and you lose some. The loss of a few battles is not the loss of the war. You still have a chance to win, if you give it another try.

"Defeat is not the worst of failures. Not to have tried is the true failure."
                                        ~George E. Woodberry

Perseverance

Trying to motivate his players to persevere through a difficult season, a college basketball coach asks his players. "Did Michael Jordan ever quit?" The team responds, "No!" Again he yells "What about the Wright Brothers?" "No!" Responds the team again. "Did John McMorran ever quit?" There was a long silence. Then the coach yells even louder. "Of course, you cannot possibly know him. He quit."
Source: Speaker's Source Book II

"You become a champion by fighting one more round. When things are tough, you fight one more round."
~ James J. Corbett

"In times like these, it helps to recall that there have always been times like these."
~Paul Harvey

"Great spirits have always encountered violent opposition from mediocre minds."
~Albert Einstein

13

You Are Being Tested

Challenges are not the cause of your failure, you are. Your challenges can only stop you temporarily, only you can stop yourself permanently.

Every now and then, you will be confronted by setbacks. Understand that whatever you are going through is just a test you must pass; a test, which is designed to question your faith, your character, your commitment.

Turn back and the message will be clear on how much faith you possess, on how committed you are, and on how puny your spirit can be.

"The trouble with some people is that during trying times they stop trying."
~*Anonymous*

Footprints

One night a man had a dream. He dreamed he was walking along the beach with the God. Across the sky flashed scenes from his life. For each scene, he noticed two sets of footprints in the sand: one belonging to him, and the other to the God.

When the last scene of his life flashed before him, he looked back at the footprints in the sand. He noticed that many times along the path of his life there was only one set of footprints. He also noticed that it happened at the very lowest and saddest times in his life.

This really bothered him and he questioned the God about it. "God, you said that once I decided to follow you, you'd walk with me all the way. But I have noticed that during the most troublesome times in my life, there is only one set of footprints. I don't understand why when I needed most, you would leave me."

The God replied, "My son, I would never leave you. During your times of trial and suffering, when you see only one set of footprints, it was then that I carried you."
Author: Mary Stevenson Parker

"I know God will not give me anything I can't handle. I just wish that He didn't trust me so much."
~Mother Teresa

message

14

Being Proactive

Why fix that which is not broken, improve on that which already works, or go further than what you have already gone?

Must you wait until your teeth turn yellow to be concerned about their whiteness, until you become ill to pay attention to your health, or until your relationships fall apart to pay attention to your significant others?

There are things that once they break, you cannot fix. If you don't constantly improve upon the status quote, it will collapse on you. Today, pick an area of your life that is 'just fine' and make it extraordinary.

"Fix it before it breaks."

~Rosa Carusone

The Ark

Everything I know or need to know, I learned from Noah's Ark

ONE: Plan ahead. It wasn't raining when Noah built the Ark.
TWO: Your hard work today will keep you from drowning tomorrow.
THREE: Stay fit. You may be asked to do something big.

FOUR: Ignore critics; get on with the job that needs to be done.
FIVE: We are all in the same boat.
SIX: When you're stressed, float awhile.

SEVEN: For safety's sake, travel in pairs.
EIGHT: The Ark was built by amateurs; the Titanic by Pros.
NINE: Don't miss the boat.
TEN: No storm last forever.
~Author Unknown

"An adventure is only an inconvenience rightly considered. An inconvenience is only an adventure wrongly considered."
~G.K. Chesterton

"What we have done for ourselves alone dies with us. What we have done for others and the world remains and is immortal."
~A. Pine

"Let the footprints of your past become the stepping stones of your present."
~Rose Dynoske

message

15

Don't Stop Now

So things might not be working out exactly the way you expected, they might not even be coming out according to plans. So what.

Trying once more might hurt, but it will hurt far less than quitting, far less than withdrawing, far less than backing out. For if you stop now, all of the sweat you have poured, all of the sacrifices you have made, and all of the time you have invested will be for nothing.

If you stop now, you might end up right where you are today. Is that good news or bad news?

"If you get up one more time than you fall you will make it through."
                                        ~Chinese Proverb

Two Sailors

Two sailors ran into each other in a bay. One of them shared about his last voyage, "After months of searching island after island for treasures with no luck, our crew wanted to abandon the search and go home. So we did."

"On our way back, we were hit by a horrendous storm. Because of the wind, we were blown onto a reef, which cracked our ship and left us stranded in an island we had no knowledge of."

"How unlucky!" Exclaimed the other sailor. "That's what I thought too. But while at this unknown island, unexpectedly, we stumbled into a treasure."
~Author Unknown

"Trust that what happened, happened for a reason. There are no accidents in life."
~Andres Lara

"Success is only one step beyond failure."
~Unknown

"If one does not know to which port one is sailing, no wind is favorable."
~Seneca

Now Is The Time

16

Time will never be just right. If you are to do something, you need to do it now whether you are ready or not.

Do what you have to do, even when you lack motivation; even when you lack preparation; even when you lack support. Do it now because no other time will be better to do what you have to do than now.

If you are to make something happen, you need to make it happen now, with whatever little training, motivation, or support you have. Whether you agree or not, now is the time.

"There are things today that you wished you had started them a year ago. Yet a year from now, there will be things that you would have wished you started today. "

~Dr. Rob Gilbert

Time: Quotes

"Time is definitely the best teacher that human beings have, yet it kills all its disciples."
~Unknown

"Do not wait; the time will never be 'just right.' Start where you stand, and work with whatever tools you may have at your command, and better tools will be found as you go along."
~Napoleon Hill

"The best way to escape from a problem is to solve it."
~Alan Saporta

"Everything in this life takes longer than you think except life itself."
~Source Unknown

"Not everything that is faced can be changed; but nothing can be changed until it is faced."
~James Baldwin

message

17

Endure A Little Longer

It's always darkest before the dawn, yet very few of us hardly ever get beyond life's obscured moments.

Realize that every night ends with a day. If you are not seeing light in your life, it's not because there is none, but rather because you refuse to go where that light can be found, beyond your darkest moments.

If you endure darkness a little longer, past where the average person stops, you'll get to see what only a handful of people have seen...light.

"You cannot see the light at the END of the tunnel if you turn around half way. Go till the end...where the light can be seen."

~Andres Lara

Winners Versus Losers

The Winner is always a part of the answer;
The Loser is always a part of the problem.

The Winner always has a plan;
The Loser always has an excuse.

The Winner says, "I'll take care of it."
The Loser says, "That's not my job."

The Winner sees an answer for every problem;
The Loser sees a problem in every answer.

The Winner says, "It may be difficult but it's possible;"
The Loser says, "It may be possible but it's too difficult."
~Author Unknown

*"Obstacles are opportunities for winners and
excuses for losers."*
~A.W.

*"The difference between winners and losers is that winners do
the little things that losers don't want to do."*
~Author Unknown

"To finish first, you must first finish."
~ Rick Mears

message

The Final Say

18

You can use the rocky experiences that life puts on your way as stumbling blocks or stepping-stones.

Bitter occurrences will emerge in your life. You have no initial say. Yet you do have the final say. Because what you add to such bitter events will determine the final taste.

Remember, it's what you add to the lemon that will make or not make lemonade. Add wisely.

"What can you add to your current bitter circumstances to make them as sweet as a lemonade?"

~Andres Lara

Post-It Notes

Some years ago, Art Fry dealt with a small irritation every Sunday as he sang in the church choir. After marking his pages in the hymnal with small bits of paper, the small pieces would invariably fall out all over the floor.

Suddenly, Art remembered an adhesive developed by a colleague that everyone thought was a failure because it did not stick very well.

He coated the adhesive on a paper sample and found that it was not only a good bookmark, but it was also great for writing notes. It will stay in place as long as he wanted it to, and then he can remove it without damage.

The resulting product was called Post-it, which has become one of 3M's most successful office products.
~Author Unknown

"Every successful man I have heard of has done the best he could with conditions as he found them."
~ Edgar Watson Howe

"Don't forget that you can always turn things around by how you react to them."
~Andres Lara

19

Start or Stop

As we all know, successful people are those who are constantly doing the little things that failures refuse to do.

Whether it's to wake up a few minutes earlier or stay up a few minutes later, whether it's to take fewer snacks at break or fewer breaks to snack.

Your success will be primarily determined by the little things you do or fail to do. What can you start or stop doing today that would better the quality of your life?

"The haves and have nots can often be traced back to the dids and did nots."
                                                                    ~Unknown

Letting Go

To let go doesn't mean to stop caring. It means I can't do it for someone else. To let go is not to cut myself off. It's the realization that I can't control another. To let go is not to enable, but to allow learning from natural consequences.

To let go is to admit powerlessness, which means the outcome is not in my hands. To let go is not to try and change or blame another, I can only change myself. To let go is not to care for, but to care about.

To let go is not to fix, but to be supportive. To let go is not to judge, but to allow another to be a human being. To let go is not to be in the middle arranging all the outcomes, but to allow others to affect their own outcomes. To let go is not to be protective, it is to permit another to face reality

To let go is not to deny, but to accept. To let go is not to nag, scold, or argue, but to search out my own shortcomings and correct them. To let go is not to adjust everything to my desires, but to take each day as it comes and cherish the moment.

To let go is not to criticize and regulate anyone, but to try to become what I dream I can be. To let go is not to regret the past, but to grow and live for the future. To let go is to fear less and love more
~Author Unknown

"The more of the past you carry around, the less of the present there is room for."
~Dalton Roberts

"You are never upset for the reason you think."
~A Course in Miracles

The Power of a Single Step

20

You will never succeed at anything unless you begin, unless you give the very first step.

The reason why so many people never succeed is not because of a lack of a vision or a dream, nor because of a lack of knowledge, but rather because of a lack of action.   One step is all the action you must take not only to begin your journey, but also to finish it.

Do not focus on the length of your journey, but simply on the power of a single step. One step will get you started, one step will build momentum, one step will lead you to the end.

"Remember, the journey of a thousand miles begins with a single step, it's continued with a single step, and it's finished with a single step."
                                                                ~Andres Lara

Take An Action

A man who had spent his life devoted to supporting his family was told he had only a few weeks to live. He feared his family would soon be in trouble without his financial assistance.

He prayed "Please God, let me win the Lottery to help my family." Day after day, he prayed but nothing came of it.

Finally he was near death, "Why, God, did you not help me?" There was silence for awhile. Then a great voice from above slowly replied, "To win the lottery, you must first buy a ticket."
~Author Unknown

"Some people wait so long for their ship to come in that their pier collapses."
~John Goddard

"You miss 100% of the shots you never take."
~Wayne Dretzky, Hockey Player

"What would you attempt to do if you knew you could not fail?"
~Dr. Robert Schuller

message

21

Feel In Charge

Life will blow against you. Don't resist its flow, because what you resist will persist.

You cannot control the fact that the wind is blowing north when you are going south, yet you can control your sails. You cannot control where you start, yet you have absolute control of your actions and, therefore, of where you end up.

What you focus on expands. Dwell on what you cannot control and you'll feel powerless; dwell on what you CAN control and you'll feel in charge.

"You cannot prevent the birds of sorrow from flying over your head, but you can prevent them from building nests in your hair."

~Chinese Proverb

Stress Prevention Kit

Rubber band: To remind you to be flexible and to stretch your ideas, and your mind to new limits, so you reach your potential.

Tissue: To remind you that's ok to cry.

Life Savors: To remind you to think of your friends as "Life Savers" who will help you through stressful times.

Candy Kiss: To remind you that everyone needs a hug, a kiss, and a word of kindness and encouragement each day.

Penny: To remind you to value your thoughts both big and small. Share what you feel you need to with others.

Eraser: To remind you that we all make mistakes, which can be erased. Also to remind you the importance of starting daily with a clean slate.

Tooth pick: To remind you to "Pick Out" the good qualities in others and yourself and to be tolerant and accepting of others.

Band Aid: To heal hurt feelings....both yours and others.

Paper Clip: It is important to keep it all together. Find balance physically, professionally and spiritually.   *~Author Unknown*

"What consumes your mind, controls your life."
~Creed

"The act of resisting something is the act of granting it life, the more you resist something, the more you make it real."
~Neale Donald Walsh

Soar To The Top

22

Like attracts like. If you want to attract success, you must be the embodiment of success.

Remember, birds of a feather flock together. If your plumage is like that of a turkey, then you cannot expect to fly like an eagle, nor can you expect to soar like one.

Pluck every feather, thought, or action which doesn't exemplify that of an eagle. If you hold on to your turkey mentality, you will get turkey results. What action can you take today to soar like an eagle?

"It's not your position, but rather your disposition which will determine your acquisition."   *~Andres Lara*

No Matter What I Win

A little boy was overheard talking to himself as he strode through his backyard, baseball cap in place and toting ball and bat. "I'm the greatest baseball player in the world." He said proudly.

Then he tossed the ball in the air, swung and missed. Undaunted, he picked up the ball, threw it into the air and said to himself, "I'm the greatest baseball player ever!" He swung at the ball again, and again he missed.

He paused a moment to examine the bat and ball carefully. Then once again he threw the ball into the air and said, "I'm the greatest baseball player who ever lived." He swung the bat hard and again missed the ball. "Wow!" he exclaimed. "What a pitcher!"

~Author Unknown

"Good Timber does not grow with ease; the stronger the wind, the stronger the trees."
~J. Willard Marriott

"You attract hearts by the qualities you display; you retain them by the qualities you possess."
~Suard

23

Comfort

Your success is in direct proportion to the level of discomfort you are willing to embrace. Are you too comfortable?

Comfort resides in what you have already mastered. Yet it's not in mastery where growth occurs, but in the journey to it. You will never grow, unless you step beyond the land of familiarity.

Dare to venture to unknown territories; for it is such journey which will not only stretch you, but will also help you discover who you really are. Trading growth for comfort, it's suicide.

"A scholar who cherishes the love of comfort is not fit to be deemed a scholar."

~Lao-Tzu

Comfort Can Cost

Once there was a beautiful bird, which flew freely across the skies. It was very proud of its freedom but it was always restless for it had no place to lie still.

One day the bird decided to pluck its own feathers, one by one, to make a beautiful nest in which it could rest with comfort and security. Now the bird had comfort, but it could no longer fly.

Author: Brian Cavanaugh, T.O.R.
Source: More Sower's Seeds

"No amount of security is worth the suffering of a life chained to a routine that has killed your dreams."
~Unknown

"There is always a price to pay for comfort. What price are you paying?"
~Andres Lara

"Our dilemma is that we hate change and love it at the same time; what we want is for things to remain the same but get better"
~Sydney Harris

Develop Character

24

There is an Irish Proverb that says, 'You've got to do your own growing, no matter how tall your grandfather was.'

Sure. There are some who were born with more than you. There are others whose lives are easier than yours. Yet all of this means nothing, for they too have to do their own growing.

Skill cannot be developed through quietness and ease, for no skillful sailor was ever developed in a calm sea. Today, choose to be ok about any turbulence you may encounter, through it you'll develop character.

"Character cannot be developed in ease and quiet. Only through the experience of trial and suffering can the soul be strengthened, ambition inspired, and success achieved." *~Helen Keller*

Things You Can Learn From A Dog

1-Never pass up the opportunity to go for a joy ride.
2-When loved ones come home, always run to greet them.
3-When it's in your best interest, practice obedience.
4-Let others know when they've invaded your territory.
5-Run, romp and play daily.
6-Be loyal.
7-If what you want lies buried, dig until you find it.
8-Avoid biting when a simple growl will do.
9-When you're happy, dance around and wag your entire body.
10-No matter how often you're scolded, don't buy into guilt
run right back and make friends.
11-Never pretend to be something you're not.
12-Stretch before rising.
13-When someone is having a bad day, be silent, sit close by
and nuzzle them gently.
~Author Unknown

"Ability may get you to the top, but it takes character to keep you there."
~John Wooden

"You can easily judge the character of a man by how he treats those who can do nothing for him."
~James D. Miles

"The measure of your real character is what you would do if you knew you would never be found out."
~Unknown

25

Higher Your Aim

When an Olympic runner aspires to break a world record and falls short, one of the worst things that can happen is receiving a gold medal.

Gold medalists usually don't aim for medals; they aim to break records. They don't train for events; they train to be the event. They don't race for victory; they race to make history.

While it's possible to get silver when you aim for gold, it's nearly impossible to get gold when you aim for silver. If you want the gold, you must aim a little higher.

"You can easily manage the difficult when you train for the impossible."
                                                        ~Andres Lara

Failed Yet Won

During the Sydney 2000 Olympics, a young athlete set an extremely high goal, to win 5 gold medals.

Yet she failed. She didn't win five gold medals. She only won three gold and two bronze. An unmatchable record. Who is she? Marion Jones.

Moral: *Set a goal that will have you win even if you fail.*

"It doesn't matter how many people say it cannot be done or how many people have tried it before; it's important to realize that whatever you are doing, it's your first attempt at it."
~Wally 'Famous' Amos

26

Not Over Yet

If you bid on a horse race, you wouldn't judge whether you won or lost until the race is over...until the end.

In the race of life at times you will find yourself sprinting, other times walking, and some other times crawling. Understand that no matter what position you find yourself in, your race is not over until the end.

Do not be quick to judge whether you have succeeded or failed. Any judgment on the race of life prior to the end will not only be inaccurate but also foolish.

"If the creator doesn't judge you till the end of your days, nor should you."
                                                    ~Source Unknown

Moso Bamboo

The moso is a bamboo plant that grows in China and the far east. After the moso is planted, no visible growth occurs for up to five years - even under ideal conditions!

Then, as if by magic, it suddenly begins growing at the rate of nearly two and one half feet per day, reaching a full height of ninety feet within six weeks.

But it's not magic. The moso's rapid growth is due to the miles of roots it develops during those first five years, five years of getting ready.

Author Unknown
Source: Sower's Seed

*"Just because you haven't reached maximum height
in so many years, it doesn't mean that
you cannot do it in a few weeks."*
~Andres Lara

*"It is no use waiting for your ship to come in unless you have
sent one out."*
~ Belgian Proverb

message

27

Take Care of The One Alive

Imagine a farmer whose livelihood depends on his two cows' milk. One day, a virus kills one of them. Destroyed by such tragedy, the farmer grieves for months. Because of his negligence, the second cow also dies.

Tragedies are inevitable. At times, you might even have to endure the loss of a beloved one. Grieve, cry if you have to, but never allow such loss to take someone else with it.

It's ok to grieve for a loss in a tragedy. Yet it's not ok to add to the tragedy by neglecting those who are still alive.

"It's not so much of a tragedy to lose somebody special, as it is to forget that special somebody who's still alive." *~Andres Lara*

Survivors

A husband, a wife and their two small children were escaping from Cuba on a small boat. The waves were approximately three to four stories high. This caused one of their children to fall off the boat. The ferocious ocean in no time swallowed the fallen kid into its debts.

The father, upset and discouraged by such tragedy, put the paddles down, sat on a corner of the boat, and burst into tears for hours.

With the boat almost sinking, the wife took the paddles in one hand and their only left child on the other one, and said to the husband, "Yes, we lost one of our dear children. And if we don't get up and row this boat through this storm, we are going to lose the one that still alive."

"In three words I can sum up everything I've learned about life - it goes on."
~Robert Frost

"Rise above the storm and you will find the sunshine."
~Mario Fernandez

"YIN-YANG: In the black, there is some white; In the wrong, there is some right; In the dark, there is some light; In the blind, there is some sight."
~Abhinyana.

message

28

Are You Ready?

An army that never trains its soldiers is easily crushed during wartime; for they will be training in the midst of combat.

It doesn't matter if you are a soldier; it doesn't matter if you have no profession. You know what your heart has longed for years. Would you be ready for it, if it shows up unexpectedly? If you are not, somebody else will.

Sharpen your skills. For your time will come. It's nearer than you think. Don't get caught off guard.

"Dig your well before you get thirsty, for a dehydrating being is in no condition to dig anything but a grave."

~*Andres Lara*

A New Champion

Two young amateur boxers were getting ready for their first professional fight. One of them could not make it to the fight.

The promoters summoned the world champion to fight the young contender. With a week notice, the champion accepted to fight. Surprisingly, the young amateur wins. The champion's excuse, "I wasn't ready."

Would you be ready if the opportunity which you most desire knocks on your door today?

"Chance favors only the prepared minds."
~Louis Pasteur

"Let us show, not merely in great crises, but in every day affairs of life, qualities of practical intelligence, of hardihood and endurance, and above all, the power of devotion to a lofty ideal."
~Theodore Roosevelt

message

29

A Known Secret

Others will love you not necessarily because of who you are, but because of how you make them feel.

Make others feel important and you will be important to them. Appreciate the little things they do, do the little things they appreciate, and you will be appreciated by them.

At times, listening does a better job than explaining, than justifying, than defending. Remember, if you fight fire with fire you will end up with ashes.

"An eye for an eye can only leave the whole world blind."
~Mahatma Gandhi

Make Others Feel Wonderful

"Mom, you were right. When I am with John I feel like he's the most wonderful person in the world. But I am not getting married to him," said Angie.

"I don't understand," said her mom.

"Mom, it's simple. I don't want to marry the most wonderful person in the world. I want to marry a guy who makes ME feel like I'm the most wonderful person in the world."

~Told By Dr. Robert Gilbert

"Remember you are just an extra in everyone else's play."
~ Stewart Emery

"The best way to sell yourself to others is first to sell the others to yourself. Check yourself against this list of obstacles to a pleasing personality: interrupting others; sarcasm; vanity; being a poor listener; insincere flattery; finding fault; challenging others without good cause; giving unsolicited advice; complaining; attitude of superiority; envy of others' success; poor posture and dress."
~Native American Proverb

message

30

Create A Master Piece

The most successful people in the world share one thing in common. They all had ONE masterpiece.

Thomas Edison held many patents but he was worldwide known for the light bulb. Leonardo Da Vinci painted many portraits but he's most known for Mona Lisa. Christopher Columbus explored and discovered many islands, but America was his masterpiece.

Why chase sardines, when a whale can satiate your hunger many times over. What masterpiece can you create that the world can know you for?

"Catch sardines and you will eat for a day, catch ONE whale and you will eat for a lifetime."   ~*Robert E. Criner*

Ballad Singer

A dramatic ballad singer studied under a strict teacher who insisted that he rehearse day after day, month after month the same passage from the same song, without being permitted to go any further. Finally, overwhelmed by frustration and despair, the young man ran off to find another profession. One night, stopping at an inn, he stumbled upon a recitation contest.

Having nothing to lose, he entered the competition and, of course, sang the one passage that he knew so well. When he had finished, the sponsor of the contest highly praised his performance. Despite the student's embarrassed objections, the sponsor refused to believe that he had just heard a beginner perform. "Tell me," the sponsor said, "who is your instructor? He must be a great master." The student later became known as the great performer Koshiji.

~Source: A Zen Story To Tell Your Neighbor

"Life is similar to a good book. The further you get into it, the more it begins to make sense."
~Harold S. Kushner

Hope

31

There is a sure way to not despair...do not hope. Yet what is life without hope?

To hope for a better tomorrow is to risk despair. To hope for light when there is nothing but darkness is to risk disappointment. To hope for success when there is nothing but failure is to risk disillusionment.

You can afford to lose your patience, your youth, and even your possessions. Yet there is only one thing that you cannot afford to lose...and that is hope.

"To the sick, while there is life there is hope."
~*Marcus T. Cicero*

Hope: Quotes

"Most of the important things in the world have been accomplished by people who have kept on trying when there seemed to be no hope at all."
~Dale Carnegie

"Hope never abandons you; you abandon it."
~George Weinberg

"Those who do not hope to win have already lost."
~ Jose Joaquin Olmedo

"Hope is the companion of power, and mother of success; for those who hope strongly have within them the gift of miracles."
~ Samuel Smiles

"Learn from yesterday, live for today, hope for tomorrow."
~Anon.

message

32

Just In Case

What would you do if you knew that today was the last day that you were going to see your significant others?

Would you give them an extra hug? Would you forgive them for yesterday's annoyance? What about running to the door before they leave and saying one more "I love you"?

The fact is that you would never know when the last day might be. But just in case, do those little things anyway for you will forever regret not doing them if the unexpected happens.

"Tomorrow is promised to no one"

~Unknown

Slow Down

Have you ever watched kids on a merry-go-round? Or listened to the rain slapping on the ground? Ever followed a butterfly's erratic flight? Or gazed at the sun into the fading night? You better slow down. Don't dance so fast. Time is short. The music won't last.

Do you run through each day on the fly? When you ask "How are you?" do you hear the reply? When the day is done, do you lie in your bed, with the next hundred chores running through your head? You better slow down. Don't dance so fast. Time is short. The music won't last.

Ever told your child, "We'll do it tomorrow"? And in your haste, not see his/her sorrow? Ever lost touch, let a good friendship die, 'Cause you never had time to call and say "Hi"? You better slow down. Don't dance so fast. Time is short. The music won't last.

When you run so fast to get somewhere you miss half the fun of getting there. When you worry and hurry through your day, it is like an unopened gift....thrown away. Life is not a race. Do take it slower. Hear the music before the song is over.   ~*Author Unknown*

"The greatest weakness of most humans is their hesitancy to tell others how much they love them while they're alive."
~*O. Battista*

"Don't forget that the business of life is not business, but living."
~*B.C. Forbes*

"The work will wait while you show the child the rainbow but the rainbow won't wait while you do the work."
~*Unknown*

Make The Most

33

If life is 10% what happens to you and 90% how you react to it; then your reaction can make what happened look like a carnival or a funeral.

Don't allow what happened to bring you down; instead use it as a wake up call, as a realization, as a reminder of what it's really important.

Just remember that what happened is not as important as how you react to it. You certainly cannot reverse the past, nor predict the future, but you can always make the most out of the present by how you react to it.

"The real winners in life are the people who look at every situation with an expectation that they can make it work or make it better."
                                        ~ Barbara Pletcher

It Can Always Be Worse

A man gets a telephone call from a doctor. The doctor says: "About this medical test I did on you, I have some good news and some bad news."

The man asks for the good news first: "The good news is that you have 24 hours to live," says the doctor. The man, incredulously says, "If that is the good news, then what is the bad news??"
"I couldn't reach you yesterday."

Source: Unknown

"I had no shoes and complained, until I met a man who had no feet."
~Indian Proverb

"Make the most of all that comes and the least of all that goes."
~Source Unknown

"It is not the situation that makes you, but it's you who make the situation."
~Frederick W. Robertson

Master The Lessons

34

There are no mistakes in life, only lessons. Resist learning these lessons and they will repeat until they are learned.

Think of life as a school. You won't move on to the next level unless you have mastered your current one. If you want to move on, you must learn whatever there's to be learned from your current situation, only then can you move forward.

Life's lessons are subtle; they will teach you about appreciation through scarcity, about discipline through temptation, and about beauty through ugliness. What can you learn from your actual situation?

"There is no shortcut to life. To the end of our days, life is a lesson imperfectly learned." ~*Harrison E. Salisbury*

Rules Of Being Human

1- You will learn lessons.

You may like the lessons or think they're irrelevant and stupid.

2. A lesson is repeated until learned.

Lessons will be presented to you in various forms. You can move forward only after you have learned the lesson.

3. Learning lessons does not end.

If you are alive, there are lessons to be learned.

4. There are no mistakes.

The "failed" experiments are as much a part of the process as the experiment that ultimately "works."

Author: Chérie Carter-Scott, Ph.D.

"Life is a succession of lessons, which must be lived to be understood."
~Ralph Waldo Emerson

"Some of us learn from other people's mistakes. The rest of us are the other people."
~Unknown

" Life is learning from our mistakes as well as our successes. The only real mistake in life is the mistake not learned from."
~Unknown

35

See For Yourself

How would you know what's possible and what's not? You will never know unless you venture out.

If you were to live behind bars for the rest of your life, you may want to check that such bars actually exist. Refuse to take someone else's word for it; perhaps such bars are no longer vertical.

At times what others have seen or thought they saw will be totally different to what you will see. Venture out and see for yourself.

"If someone tells you that you cannot do something and you believe it, they are right."   *~Carol Burnett*

Never Follow A Costume Blindly

The new husband watched his wife prepare her first ham for the oven and noticed that she cut off a few inches from one end and asked why she did that, she replied that her mother always did it the same way. They called mother, and while she admitted always cutting off a few inches, she could give no reason except that her mother had always done it. Finally, they called grandma, and she explained: "Oh, I always did that because my pan was too small."
Source: That Reminds Me, C. Publishing House

"Never accept others' limitations as your own. For they might not apply to you." ~Andres Lara

"From my tribe I take nothing I am the maker of my own fortune." ~Tecumseh

"Our lives begin to end the day we start becoming silent about things that matter." ~Unknown

"People see the world not as it is, but as they are." ~Al Lee

Illusion of Knowledge

36

At times, you must disregard the fact that others have failed in the past at what you want to attempt on the present.

Imagine a warden who gives a key to a prisoner to help him escape. After a few tries, the inmate gives up. The key didn't work. Unaware of the past, a year later, another prisoner tries the key and opens the lock.

Keep in mind that the illusion of knowing what works or doesn't work is the only thing keeping you from liberating yourself.

"What would you attempt to do today if you didn't know what you know about your limitations?"   ~Andres Lara

Not Knowing

"Homework. It's impossible for you to solve, but experiment with it," instructed a math teacher as she wrote on the board an equation for her fourth grade class. John, one of her students, missed what the teacher had said but saw the equation on the board, wrote it down, and took it home.

While at home, John noticed that he had never learned how to solve this kind of equations. So he went to the library, read some math's books, and solved the equation. The next day, he showed the solved equation to the teacher to which she replied "Impossible."

Told by Dr. Robert Gilbert

"Everything is possible as long as you don't know that it's impossible."
~Andres Lara

"The impossible is often the untried."
~John Goodwin

"Do not let what you cannot do interfere with what you can do."
~John Wooden

"Give a me a fish and I'll eat for a day. Teach me how to fish and I'll eat for a lifetime."
~Ancient Proverb

message

37

Still Ticking

How do you know when to stop playing the game of life? How do you know when to stop thriving for victory?

No matter what's the score, a football game is not over until the clock stops ticking. Similarly, if your biological clock is still running, then your game is not over yet.

Keep in mind that as long as your clock is ticking, you still have playtime and, therefore, a chance to win.

"It's not over until it's over."

~*Author Unknown*

Perseverance: Quotes

"Life was meant to be lived, and curiosity must be kept alive. You must never, for whatever reason, turn your back on life."
~Eleanor Roosevelt

"The wayside of business is full of brilliant people who started out with a spurt, and lacked the stamina to finish. Their places were taken by patient and unshowy plodders who never knew when to quit."
~ J. R. Todd

"Keep on going and the chances are that you will stumble on something, perhaps when you are least expecting it. I have never heard of anyone stumbling on something sitting down."
~Charles F. Kettering

"History has demonstrated that the most notable winners usually encountered heartbreaking obstacles before they triumphed. They won because they refused to become discouraged by their defeats."
~ B. C. Forbes

There's Always A Reason

38

Everything happens for a reason. Though this reason might not always be visible, know that there is always a reason behind what happened.

Think about the poor farmer who spent his entire life's savings on a ticket to get on Titanic, but missed the boat. He was upset. He was enraged. He was fuming. Until he heard...Titanic sank.

Don't be quick to assume a position of misery for what's currently happening in your life. Time will prove that there was a reason behind what happened.

"Nothing happens without a reason."   ~Andres Lara

The Burning Hut

The only survivor of a shipwreck washed up on a small, uninhabited island. He prayed feverishly for God to rescue him, and every day he scanned the horizon for help, but none seemed forthcoming. Exhausted, he eventually managed to build a little hut out of driftwood to protect him from the elements and to store his few possessions. But then one day, after scavenging for food, he arrived home to find his little hut in flames, with the smoke rolling up to the sky. The worst had happened; everything was lost.

He was stung with grief and anger. "God, how could you do this to me!" he cried. Early the next day, however, he was awakened by the sound of a ship that was approaching the island. It had come to rescue him. "How did you know I was here?" asked the weary man of his rescuers. "We saw your smoke signal," they replied.

~Author Unknown

"Never forget that blessings do come in disguise."
~Unknown

"Our greatest glory consists not in never falling, but in rising every time we fall."
~Confucius

39

Unshakable Inner Peace

With so much going on in your life and around the world how can you experience inner peace?

Inner peace evolves from having your actions in harmony with your beliefs...that is doing what you believe is right at all times, pursuing what's important, and being unwilling to settle for anything less.

It's only when your actions contradict your beliefs that your inner peace is shaken. Only you know what's right and important to you; do those things and your inner peace will be unshakable.

"The truth of the matter is that we always know the right thing to do. The challenge is in doing it." *~Norman Schwarzkopf*

Inner Peace Portrait

There once was a King who offered a prize to the artist who would paint the best picture of peace. Many artists tried. The King looked at all the pictures, but there were only two he really liked and he had to choose between them. One picture was of a calm lake. The lake was a perfect mirror, for peaceful towering mountains were all around it. Overhead was a blue sky with fluffy white clouds. All who saw this picture thought it was a perfect picture of peace. The other picture had mountains, too. But these were rugged and bare. Above was an angry sky from which rain fell, and in which lightening played.

Down the side of the mountain tumbled a foaming waterfall. This did not look peaceful at all. But when the King looked, he saw behind the waterfall a tiny bush growing in a crack in the rock. In the bush a mother bird had built her nest. There, in the midst of the rush of angry water, sat the mother bird on her nest. The King chose the second picture. "Because," explained the King, "peace does not mean to be in a place where there is no noise, trouble, or hard work. Peace means to be in the midst of all those things and still be calm in your heart. That is the real meaning of peace."   ~*Author Unknown*

"Peace emerges in your life when you can find silence within in spite of the noise without."   ~*Andres Lara*

"For peace of mind, we need to resign as general manager of the universe."   ~*Larry Eisenberg*

"Maturity is the ability to live in peace with that which you cannot change."   ~*Ann Landers*

message

40

Ambition

No great accomplishment has ever been attained without an ambitious person behind it.

Ambition is the ability to expect more out of life than others think is feasible, to risk more than others think is safe, to dream more than others think is realistic.

If ambition is all you have, ambition is all you will need. For time and time again, big accomplishments are attained by an average person who is ambitious enough to aim above the average.

"Big results require big ambitions."
                                    ~James Champy

Ambition: Quotes

"Intelligence without ambition is like a bird
without wings."
~ *C. Archie Danielson*

"When you go in search of honey you must expect to be
stung by bees."
~ *Kenneth Kaunda*

"Ambition is not a vice of little people."
~*Michel de Montaigne*

"All right Mister, let me tell you what winning means... you're
willing to go longer, work harder, give more than anyone else."
~ *Vince Lombardi*

"God gave you limited ability,
But unlimited ambition and desire."
~*Author unknown*

Desire

41

If you desire a dream intensively enough, there's nothing that can stand in your way.

You must desire your dreams as bad as a drowning person desires air, as bad as a starving person desires food, as bad as a homeless person desires shelter.

Once you develop a strong desire for what you want, there will be no mountain that you cannot climb, no obstacle that you cannot surpass, no distance that you cannot endure.

"Desire! That's the one secret of everyone's career. Not education. Not being born with hidden talents. Desire."

~Bobby Unser

How Much Do You Want It

The story is told that a young man asked Socrates how he could get wisdom. "Come with me," Socrates replied. He took the lad to a river and shoved his head underwater. He held it there until the boy struggled for air. Then he let him go.

Once the boy regained his composure, Socrates asked him, "What did you desire most when your head was underwater?" "I wanted air," the boy told him. Socrates nodded slowly. "When you want wisdom as much as you wanted air when you were immersed in the water," he said "you will receive it."

Source: (book) The Power Of Your Subconscious Mind

"If you care enough for a result, you will most certainly attain it."
~William James

"We are told that talent creates its own opportunities. But it sometimes seems that intense desire creates not only its own opportunities, but its own talents." ~Eric Hoffer

"The starting point of all achievement is desire. Keep this constantly in mind. Weak desires bring weak results, just as a small amount of fire makes a small amount of heat."
~Napoleon Hill

message

42

Enthusiasm

When the going gets tough, the tough must not only get going but get going with enthusiasm.

In life, everyone has to go through peaks and valleys. If you remain enthusiastic while going through your lowest point, your distance will become shorter, your burden lighter, and your path smoother.

Remember, no great achiever has ever lack enthusiasm. To get far in life you must be as enthusiastic about your failures as you are about your successes.

"Success consists of going from failure to failure without loss of enthusiasm."   *~Winston Churchill*

Human's Fuel

A newspaper reporter secured an exclusive interview with the devil. The reporter was especially interested in the deceptive techniques around which the devil had built his reputation.

'What's the most useful tool you use on people? Is it dishonesty? Envy? Anger?' Asked the reporter.

No, no, no, chuckled the devil. The most useful weapon I possess is apathy because it depletes the human spirit from its fuel...enthusiasm.
Source: Speakers' Source Book II

"Everyone is enthusiastic at times. There are those who are enthusiastic for 30 minutes, others who are for 30 days, but only those who remain enthusiastic for 30 years attain a successful life."
~Edward B. Butler

"What I do best is sharing my enthusiasm."
~Bill Gate

message

43

Start Climbing

A magnifying glass can make a tiny pebble look as big as a mountain, a little drop of water as a big as the ocean, and a small mosquito as big as a dinosaur.

Your perception can blow things out of proportion just like a magnifying glass. At times what you actually see and your perception about what you see are two different things.

What if that mountain which is preventing you from moving forward is nothing more than a tiny pebble enlarged by your perception? Find out. Start climbing.

"The eye of a human being is a microscope, which makes the world seem bigger than it really is."   *~Kahlil Gibran*

Perception: Quotes

"Reality is what we take to be true.
What we take to be true is what we believe.
What we believe is based on our perceptions.
What we perceive depends on what we look for.
What we look for depends on what we think.
What we think depends on what we perceive.
What we perceive determines what we take to be true.
What we take to be true is our reality."
~*Gary Zukav*

"All is perspective. To a worm, digging the ground is more
relaxing than going fishing."
~*Clyde Abel*

"The same lion that draws frantic tears from our eyes in the
dark jungle will have us joyfully giggle in a circus."
~*Andres Lara*

"In the kingdom of the blind, the one-eyed man is king."
~*Desiderius Erasmus, Adages*

message

44

You've Grown

If you look back at your challenges from last year, you will notice that they are not as big and as scary as they used to be.

If your past challenges seem smaller, it's not because they shrank but rather because YOU grew. You are not today, who you were yesterday; nor will you be tomorrow who you are today.

Everyday you outgrow many of your old scary challenges. Everyday you will be able to do something, which couldn't do before simply because you've grown.

"If you couldn't do something yesterday, it doesn't mean that you cannot do it today. For who you are today is not who you used to be."
~Andres Lara

I'm Still Growing

Though Edmund Hillary failed on his first attempt, on his second try he climbed to the top of Mount Everest. A few weeks after his success, he addressed a group. From the stage, he pointed at a picture of the mountain and said in a loud voice, "Mount Everest, you beat me the first time, but I beat you the second time around because you grew all you were going to grow... but I'm still growing!"
~*Brian Cavanaugh, T.O.R.,*

"Challenges are what make life interesting; overcoming them is what makes life meaningful."
~*Joshua J. Marine*

"Never measure the height of a mountain until you have reached the top then you will see how low it really was."
~*Dag Hammarskjold*

"Never let a day pass you without saying, I will do better tomorrow."
~ *Brigham Young*

message

45

Take Another Step

When every ounce of strength is drained from you, when you have given all you had to give, when your hope wears out; it's then when you must take another step forward.

One step beyond hopelessness will give you access to that which cannot be drained, taken, or worn out. That which, like the ocean, cannot be depleted...your essence.

You have more energy than challenges will ever be able to consume, more strength than you will ever be able to employ, and more to give than there is to be given. Take another step.

"Life gives anything we ask of it only after we refuse to take no for an answer."
                                                    ~Andres Lara

Hope: Quotes

"You don't drown by falling in the water; you drown by staying there."
~ *Edwin Louis Cole*

"Most of the important things in the world have been accomplished by people who have kept on trying when there seemed to be no hope at all."
~*Dale Carnegie*

"When the odds are against me I prove them wrong,
When all else fails I succeed,
When all else ceases to live I breath,
When all turns to ashes from it I rise,
So it doesn't matter what you throw at me or what you do,
I am, I do, that's all that matters."
~*Heather Griggs*

"Effort only fully releases its reward after a person refuses to quit."
~*Napoleon Hill*

"Tough times never last, but tough people do."
~ *Robert H. Schuller*

message

46

It Gets Better

When your hopes are down, as they sometimes will; when your emotional wounds seem, as though, they will never heal; when the journey you are on, seems less than ideal; it's then that you must exercise your mental will.

Tell yourself. It will get sunnier. I will get healthier and wealthier, and my journey will get easier.

At the end of your life, who knows, you might not be right. Maybe it didn't get sunnier, maybe you didn't get healthier or wealthier, and maybe your journey didn't get any easier. But at least you would be able to say that you enjoyed the ride.

"Remember, life is not about the place where you will arrive, but rather about enjoying the drive." *~Andres Lara*

Optimism: Quotes

"In the long run the pessimist may be proved right, but the optimist has a better time on the trip."
~*Daniel L. Reardon*

"The essence of optimism is that it takes no account of the present, but it is a source of inspiration, of vitality and hope where others have resigned; it enables a man to hold his head high, to claim the future for himself and not to abandon it to his enemy."
~*Dietrich Bonhoeffer*

"The point of living, and of being an optimist,
is to believe that the best is yet to come."
~*Peter Ustinov*

"An optimist may see a light where there is none, but why must the pessimist always run to blow it out?"
~ *Michel De Saint-Pierre*

"You can complain because roses have thorns, or you can rejoice because thorns have roses."
~*Ziggy*

message

47

Find It

To accomplish great things you must not only dream, but also act. Not only believe, but also risk.

You must not lose faith when everything is against you. If every door you turn to is closed, knock. If it doesn't open, find another one. If you knock enough doors, eventually one will open.

No door has ever stood in between a dreamer and a dream. If you knock every door and none opened, find a window or a chimney. There is always a way in, you must find it.

"Behold the turtle. It makes progress only when it sticks its neck out."
                                                    ~*James Bryant Conant*

Take The Stairs

A group of tourists who were visiting the Empire
State Building in New York City heard the guide
announce loudly that there was a three-hour wait
to ride the elevator to the top of the building.
However, with a smile on his face the guide then
said, "There is no one waiting to go to the top if
you are willing to take the stairs.
~Zig Zigglar

*"The elevator to success is out of order. You'll have to use the
stairs... one step at a time."*
~Joe Girard

*"If you have tried to do something and failed, you are vastly better off
than if you had tried to do nothing and succeeded. You must never
regret what might have been. The past that did not happen is as hidden from us as the future we cannot see."*
~ Richard Martin Stern

*"Failures are divided into two classes -- those who thought and never
did, and those who did and never thought."*
~ John Charles Salak

message

48

Start Today

It should not be a problem to begin at the very end of the line of success, yet it should be a problem not to begin at all.

The only way to get to the highest rung of any ladder is by beginning to climb from a lower rung. Refuse to start climbing and you will remain at the very bottom.

Where you start it's certainly not where you will end up. Yet if you never start, you will end up exactly where you are right now. Start today.

"Great beginnings are not as important as the way one finishes."
~*Dr. James Dobson*

Start: Quotes

"Our background and circumstances may influence who we are, but we are responsible for who we become."
~Unknown

"The greatest amount of wasted time is the time not getting started."
~ Dawson Trotman

"Don't wait for someone to take you under their wing. Find a good wing and climb up underneath it."
~ Frank C. Bucaro

"Putting off an easy thing makes it hard, and putting off a hard one makes it impossible."
~ George H. Lonmer

"Begin to weave and God will give the thread."
~ German Proverb

message

49

Exemplify Don't Criticize

If you want others to be a particular way, you must be that way yourself.

The best way to preach to others is by having your walk being your preaching. Rather than being critical of others, you can model the behavior you want them to perform.

People will resent your criticism, but will be influenced by your behaviors. Besides, no one loves a critic. What behavior can you exemplify today?

"Never criticize a person until you've walked a mile in his/her moccasins."   *~American Indian Proverb*

Silent Teaching

I'd rather see one sermon a week, than to hear one a day;
I'd rather one to walk with me than merely show me the way;
The eye's a better student, and more willing than the ear;
Fine counsel is confusing, but example's always clear.

Best of all the preachers are those who lived their creeds;
For to see good put into action, that is what everybody needs.
I soon can learn to do it, if you'll let me see it done;
I can see your hands in action, but your tongue too fast may run.

The lectures you deliver may be very fine and true,
But I'd rather get my lesson by observing what you do.
For I may misunderstand you and the high advice you give,
But there's no misunderstanding how you act and how you live!
~Author Unknown

"Much wisdom often goes with fewer words."
~Sophocles

"When you judge others, you do not define them, you define yourself."
~Earl Nightingale

"It is not the critic who counts, not the one who points out how others stumble or where the doer of deeds could have done them better. The credit belongs to those who are actually in the arena, whose faces are marred by dust and sweat and blood."
~Theodore Roosevelt

message

50

Let It Be Harsh

Have you ever thought that maybe there is a meaningful reason behind whatever you are currently going through?

Keep in mind that it's out of hardship that greatness is forced to emerge, creativity is compelled to perspire, and leadership is commanded to appear. Let it be harsh. The harsher it is, the sharper you will become.

Human greatness has rarely emerged out of lack of difficulties. As history reveals, great leaders, giant progress, and unrealistic accomplishments have always emerged as a response to chaos.

"Let those obstacles that paralyze many, be another reason for you to strive for greatness."   *~Andres Lara*

Difficulties: Quotes

"People are like stained-glass windows. They sparkle and shine when the sun is out, but when the darkness sets in, their true beauty is revealed only if there is a light from within."
~Elizabeth Kubler-Ross

"Triumphs without difficulties are empty. Indeed; it is difficulties that make the triumph. It is no feat to travel the smooth road."
~ Source Unknown

"Life is a blend of laughter and tears, a combination of rain and sunshine."
~Norman Vincent Peale

"It is surmounting difficulties that makes heroes."
~ Louis Kossuth

"It cannot be too often repeated that it is not helps, but obstacles, not facilities, but difficulties that make heroes."
~ William Mathews

Together

51

Getting together is important, but not as important as remaining together.

Keep in mind that the more hands you have, the lighter your work will be. The more eyes you have, the greater scope your vision will reach. The more partnerships you develop, the louder your voice will echo.

You will achieve more as a result of working with others than against them. Develop a new partnership today.

"Alone we can do so little; together we can do so much."
~*Helen Keller*

Teamwork

A father had a family of sons who were perpetually quarreling among themselves. When he failed to heal their disputes by his exhortations, he determined to give them a practical illustration of the evils of disunion; and for this purpose he one day told them to bring him a bundle of sticks. When they had done so, he placed the faggot into the hands of each of them in succession, and ordered them to break it in pieces.

They tried with all their strength, and were not able to do it. He next opened the faggot, took the sticks separately, one by one, and again put them into his sons' hands, upon which they broke them easily. He then addressed them in these words: "My sons, if you are of one mind, and unite to assist each other, you will be as this faggot, uninjured by all the attempts of your enemies; but if you are divided among yourselves, you will be broken as easily as these sticks."

~Author Unknown

"When a blind man carries a legless man, they both go forward." ~Swedish proverb

"We are each of us angels with only one wing, and we can only fly by embracing one another."
~Luciano de Crescenzo

Pick Your Own Weight

52

Trying to make the world a better place can be an overwhelming task. Where should you start?

Start by making yourself the best you can possibly be. Reach as far as you can possibly go. Live your life in such a way that others are compelled to live theirs.

Make the world's burden a little lighter by picking, lifting, and carrying your own weight.

"Do a little more each day than you think you possibly can."

~*Lowell Thomas*

Start With You

"Build a better world,"
said God. I asked, "How?
The world is such a vast
place and so complicated
now, and I'm so small,
where could I possibly
start?" God in all His
wisdom replied, "Start by
building a better you."
~Author Unknown

*"Your focus should be on eliminating the cause and not on
treating the symptoms."*
~Author Unknown

*"If you want a change in attitude, start with a change in
behavior."*
~William Glasser

*"Most bold changes are the result of a hundred thousand tiny
changes that culminate in a bold outcome."*
~Thomas Peters

"A candle loses nothing by lighting another candle."
~Unknown

message

53

Change Your Perception

You might not have the ability to change people, but you certainly have the power to change your perception about them.

If you looked at the world from behind a blue glass, everything would look blue. Even if you painted things in red; you would still see them in blue.

Likewise, people won't change merely because you try to change them; they will change only when you change the standpoint from where you are looking at them.

"Seek not to change the world, but choose to change your mind about the world." *~A Course in Miracles*

Don't Alter The World

Once upon a time, there was a king who ruled a prosperous country. One day, he went for a trip to some distant areas of his country. When he was back to his palace, he complained that his feet were very painful, because it was the first time that he went for such a long trip, and the road that he went through was very rough and stony. He then ordered his people to cover every road of the entire country with leather. Definitely, this would need thousands of cows' skin, and would cost a huge amount of money. Then one of his wise servants dared himself to tell the king, "Why do you have to spend that unnecessary amount of money? Why don't you just cut a little piece of leather to cover your feet?" The king was surprised, but he later agreed to his suggestion, to make a "pair of shoe" for himself.   *~Author Unknown*

"Everyone thinks of changing the world, but no one thinks about changing themselves."
~John Randolph

"Your attitude is a reflection of you and your world mirrors your attitude."
~Earl Nightingale

message

54

Turn It Into An Asset

There's an advantage in your current disadvantage. Nothing has ever been created for the mere purpose of hindering you.

In a world where survival of the fittest has become survival of the fastest, turtles' heavy shell could be considered a curse for it takes away their agility.

Yet it's because of their shells that turtles are not chewed by crocodiles or smashed by elephants. Shells therefore are an asset for turtles. How can your disadvantage be an asset for you?

"For every mountain there is a miracle."

~ Robert H. Schuller

The Cracked Pot

A water bearer in India had two large pots, each hung on each end of a pole which he carried across his neck. At the end of the long walk from the stream to his master's house, one pot would arrive only half full; for it was old and had a crack in it.

"I want to apologize to you," said the old cracked pot. "Why?" asked the bearer. "Because of this crack on my side, water leaks out of me from the stream all the way back to the master's house. Because of my flaw, you don't get full value from your efforts," the pot said.

To which the bearer replied, "Have you ever noticed that along the path to the master's house there are flowers only on your side of the path, but not on the other pot's side? That's because I have always known about your flaw, and I took advantage of it.

I planted flower seeds on your side of the path, and every day while we walked back from the stream, you've watered them. For two years I have been able to pick these beautiful flowers to decorate the master's table. Without you being just the way you are, the master would not have this beauty to grace his house."

~Author Unknown

"There is always a creative way to turn your weakness into a strength. Your job is to find that way."
~Andres Lara

message

55

Beyond The Obvious

Beware of what you wish for. You might very well receive it. In fact, you have received everything you have ever wanted.

Just like a gift comes concealed by wrapping paper, life's grandest and most priceless gifts will come to you under the mask of unwanted circumstances.

If you look beyond what's currently happening, beyond the obvious adversity, you'll find something of extreme value, something worth enduring for.

"To achieve the impossible, one must think the absurd; to look where everyone else has looked, but to see what no one else has seen."
~Unknown

I Received Everything

I asked God for Strength...
And He gave me difficulties to make me strong.
I asked God for Wisdom...
And He gave me problems to solve.

I asked God for Prosperity...
And He gave me brain and brawn to work.
I asked God for Courage...
And He gave me danger to overcome.

I asked God for Love...
And He gave me troubled people to help.
I asked God for Favors...
And He gave me opportunities.

I received nothing the way I wanted...
Yet I received everything.
~Author Unknown

"Don't judge each day by the harvest you reap ... but by the seeds you plant!"
~Robert Louis Stevenson

"The best and most beautiful things in the world cannot be seen or even touched. They must be felt with the heart."
~Hellen Keller

message

56

They Are Your Reflection

You cannot be certain about someone being happy, if you have never experienced happiness yourself. You cannot be certain about recognizing love, if you have never been in love yourself.

To be certain of something, you must personally know of it. If you are certain that others are selfish and righteous, this says little about their selfishness and righteousness but rather about yours.

You see who you are. If you want to see less selfish and righteous people, then you must be less selfish and righteous yourself.

"All judgment reveals itself to be self-judgment in the end, and when this is understood a larger comprehension of the nature of life takes its place."   *~David R. Hawkins*

We See What We Are

The good you find in others, is in you too. The faults you find in others, are your faults as well. After all, to recognize something you must know it. The possibilities you see in others, are possible for you as well. The beauty you see around you, is your beauty. The world around you is a reflection, a mirror showing you the person you are. To change your world, you must change yourself. To blame and complain will only make matters worse.

See the best in others, and you will be your best. Give to others, and you give to yourself. Appreciate beauty, and you will be beautiful. Admire creativity, and you will be creative. Love, and you will be loved. Seek to understand, and you will be understood. Listen, and your voice will be heard. Show your best face to the mirror, and you'll be happy with the face looking back at you.
~Author Unknown

"Don't let what other people think decide who you are."
~Dennis Rodman

"You wouldn't worry so much about what people really thought of you if you knew just how seldom they actually do."
~Unknown

57

You Are The Master

When all odds are against you. You must challenge. You must dare. You must persist. You must endure.

Remember, it's never over until it's over. And only you can say when it's over. Not your friend, not your significant others, not your boss. You.

Only you can say where the end is. How is the end going to be. And what is the end going to look like. Don't forget, you are in charge. You are the master.

"Live your own life, for you will die your own death."

~*Latin Proverb*

Life Gives What You Ask For

I bargained with Life for a penny,
And Life would pay no more
However I begged at evening
When I counted my scanty store;
For Life is a just employer,
It gives you what you ask,
But once you have set your wages,
Why you must bear the task.
I worked for a menial's hire,
Only to learn dismayed
That any wage I had asked of Life
Life would have paid.
~Jessie Rittenhouse

*"There's only one way to succeed in anything and that is to give
everything. I do and I demand that my players do. Players'
finest hours is when they have worked their hearts out in a good
cause and lye exhausted on the field of battle...victorious."*
~Vince Lombardi

*"To be yourself in a world that is constantly trying to make you
something else is the greatest accomplishment."*
~Ralph Waldo Emerson

message

58

Feel Proud

There are no extraordinary jobs; there are only ordinary jobs performed in extraordinary ways...performed with pride.

Pride doesn't come from what you do; it comes from HOW you do what you do; from what you make of what you do.

It doesn't matter what your title, position, or profession might be. It doesn't matter what others might think of your line of work. Do it like it has never been done before, do it in a way that makes YOU feel proud.

"The quality of a person's life is in direct proportion to their commitment to excellence, regardless of their chosen field of endeavor."
                                                              ~*Vince Lombardi*

Aim To Be The Best

If you can't be a pine on the top of a hill, be a scrub in the valley but be the best little scrub by the side of the hill; be a bush if you can't be a tree. If you can't be a bush, be a bit of the grass, and some highway happier make; if you can't be a muskie then just be a bass, but be the liveliest bass in the lake!

We can't all be captains, someone has to be crew. There's something for all of us here and the task we must do is near. If you can't be a highway, then just be a trail, if you can't be the sun, be a star. It isn't by size that you win or you fail. Be the best of whatever you are and you will prevail.
~Author Unknown

"Nobody who has given his/her best has ever regretted it."
~George Halas

"The only thing that stands between you and what you want is often merely the will to try it and the faith to believe that it's possible."
~Richard M. De Vos

"If you don't invest very much, then defeat doesn't hurt very much and winning is not very exciting." ~Dick Vermeil

"It's not who you are that holds you back, it's who you think you're not." ~Unknown

59

Shortcuts

No one likes to take the longest road to the top. This is why you might want to consider traveling on it.

There is always a line to take the elevator, yet there is never a line to climb up the stairs. Why wait online to do tomorrow what you can start doing and finish today.

Remember the fast and easy way to the top is desired by many, so if you decide to go on it, expect a heavy traffic.

"At times the fastest way to the top is the slowest one."

~*Andres Lara*

TheCubanGuy.com

Easy Roads Are Crowded

The easy roads are crowded,
And the level roads are jammed;
The pleasant little rivers
With the drifting folks are crammed,
But off yonder where it's rocky,
Where you get a better view,
You will find the ranks are thinning
And the travelers are few.
Where the going's smooth and pleasant
You will always find the throng,
For the many, more's the pity,
Seem to like to drift along.
But the steps that call for courage
And the task that's hard to do,
In the end results in glory
For the never-wavering few.
~Messick

*"Do not follow where the path may lead. Go instead
where there is no path and leave a trail."*
~Ralph Waldo Emerson

*"You should never judge a book by its cover; nor should
you judge it by its first chapter."*
~Unknown

"The path of least resistance is the path of the loser."
~H. G. Wells

message

60

Seek For Blessings

The same challenge that can bury you alive, can also elevate you towards the top.

For every challenge that comes your way, there's an equal, if not bigger, blessing accompanying it. Just because you don't see good things, it doesn't mean that there are none.

Remember, seek and you shall find. Seek for the blessings within your current dilemma and you'll find them.

"Blessings are only found by those who take the time to seek for them."
                                                              ~Andres Lara

Shake It Off

Two horses, who belonged to a local farmer, fell into a dried well. After carefully assessing the situation, the farmer decided the horses were not worth the trouble of saving. So, he began hauling dirt to bury the horses in the well and put them out of misery.

After several hours of a continuous rain of dirt on the horses' back, one horse steps out of the well, yet the other one was buried alive. What happened? Every time dirt landed on the back of the surviving horse...HE WOULD SHAKE IT OFF AND STEP UP!

It wasn't long before this horse stepped out of the well. The same dirt that buried one horse alive was the same dirt that elevated the surviving horse to freedom.

~Author Unknown

"It's not your current dilemma that will have you sink, it's how you react to it."
~Andres Lara

"A rock pile ceases to be a rock pile the moment you contemplate it, bearing within you the image of a cathedral."
~Antoine De Saint-Exupery

message

61

It's Time

If your surroundings are not providing a strong enough excitement for you, perhaps it is time...

It's time for you to stop following someone else's beat. It's time for you to listen to that which you have been trying to ignore...your own inner drum.

Aren't you tired of following someone else's rhythm? Aren't you tired of dancing to the beat of a slower drum?

"If you do not keep pace with those around you, perhaps it is because you hear a different drum. Step to the music that you hear."

~*Henry David Thoreau*

Conformity: Quotes

"Follow the path of the unsafe, independent thinker. Expose your ideas to the dangers of controversy. Speak your mind and fear less the label of 'crackpot' than the stigma of conformity. And on issues that seem important to you, stand up and be counted at any cost."
~Thomas J. Watson

"To be a star you must follow your own light, follow your own path, and never fear the darkness, for that is when stars shine the brightest."
~Unknown

"Conformity is the jailer of freedom and the enemy of growth."
~John F. Kennedy

"Do not seek to follow in the footsteps of the wise; seek what they sought."
~Baslo

"Everyone has talent. What is rare is the courage to follow the talent to the dark place where it leads."
~Erica Jong

A Fervent Desire

62

A fervent desire is that which has you see the invisible, believe in the incredible, and attain what many refer to as the impossible.

A fervent desire is that which has you seek fanatically, explore obsessively, and ask endlessly. That which regardless of feeling defeated, has you begin anyway.

To succeed in life, you must have more than education, more than talent, more than intellect. You must have a fervent desire.

"Dwell not upon your weariness, for your strength shall be according to the measure of your desire."

~Arabian Proverb

Join The 2% Club

My elementary school baseball coach was a very wise old man. I remember that one day during practice, he walked me to the side of the field and said "Son, look around you. Of all the people in the entire baseball league, only 10 % will go on to play high school baseball. Of that 10 %, only 5 % will continue on to play in college. Of that remaining 5%, only 2 % will play for the pros. Do you know what is the only quality separating these men?" He asked me. Then he continued, "DESIRE. You have to want to be in those 2% who have a fervent desire for the game." This principle applies to anything and everything. Only a very small percentage of people who start their own business succeed. Only a small percentage of people who aim to become wealthy succeed. And I have come to the realization that the ultimate deciding factor to everything is "DESIRE," as my old baseball coach once said.   *~Author Unknown*

"The starting point of all achievement is desire. Keep this constantly in mind. Weak desires bring weak results, just as a small amount of fire makes a small amount of heat."
~Napoleon Hill

"Steam or gas doesn't drive anything until it is confined. Niagara doesn't turn into light and power until it is tunneled. Life doesn't grow until it's focused, dedicated, and disciplined."
~Harry Emerson Fosdick

message

63

Nurture The Inner Self

Once a rose is plucked out of the garden, it dries slowly. Yet if it's kept planted, its beauty radiates for years.

Your soul needs a garden. A garden where your roots could be nurtured, your thoughts composed, and your inner-peace recaptured. Do you have such garden?

If you do, spend more time in it. If you don't, create one because without it, your inner-self will slowly dry like a rose plucked out of the garden.

"Spend intimate time with someone very special...you."

~*Andres Lara*

Children Learn

If children live with criticism, they learn to condemn;
If children live with hostility, they learn to fight;
If children live with ridicule, they learn to be shy;
If children live with shame, they learn to feel guilty;

If children live with tolerance, they learn to be patient;
If children live with encouragement, they learn confidence;
If children live with praise, they learn to appreciate;
If children live with fairness, they learn justice;

If children live with security, they learn to have faith;
If children live with approval, they learn to like themselves;
If they live with acceptance, they learn to find love in the world.
Author: Dorothy Law Holte

"It's not what you leave to your children, it's what you leave in your children." ~Unknown

"Advice is like snow; the softer it falls, the longer it dwells upon, the deeper it sinks into the mind."
~Samuel Taylor Coleridge

"We spend the first twelve months of our children's lives teaching them to walk and talk and the next twelve telling them to sit down and shut up."
~Phyllis Diller

64

Habits

Remember what it was like to learn how to walk? It was hard. It took full concentration.

Yet today you don't think about how to walk, you just walk. Since you've walked so much, it's become an unconscious habit. Think of something that's hard and you would like to do it with more ease.

All you have to do is do it more often. Do it so many times that eventually it becomes part of you. It becomes a habit. It takes twenty-one days to create a habit. What healthy habit can you start today?

"Successful people are successful because they form the habits of doing those things that failures don't like to do." *~Albert Gray*

Allied Or Enemy?

I am your constant companion.
I can be your greatest helper or heaviest burden.
I will push you to the top or drag you down to failure.
I am completely at your command. Half of the things you do,
you might just as well turn over to me,
And I will be able to do them quickly and correctly.

I am easily managed; you must merely be firm with me.
Show me exactly how you want something done,
And after a few lessons I will do it automatically.
I am the servant of all great men and of all failures as well.

Those who are great, I have made great.
Those who are failures, I have made failures.
I am not a machine, though I work with all the precision of one
Plus the intelligence of a human.

You may run me for profit, or run me for ruin;
It makes no difference to me.
Take me, train me, be firm with me
And I will put the world at your feet.
Be easy with me, and I will destroy you.
Who am I? I am HABIT!
~Author Unknown

*"We are what we repeatedly do. Excellence, then, is not an act,
but a habit."*
~Aristotle

message

65

Your Love or a Gate?

Loving someone doesn't give you the right to prevent him/her from going elsewhere.

If you really want someone to stay with you, you should not keep him/her as a prisoner. If you have to keep a person gated, like a wild animal in the zoo, to prevent him/her from escaping you then that person doesn't deserve your time nor your love.

Open the gate. If the person stays, at least you know that's your love and not a gate, which is making him/her stay.

"If you love something let it go free. If it doesn't come back, you never had it. If it comes back, love it forever." ~*Author unknown*

Love: Quotes

"Love may be blind, but it can sure find its way around the dark!"
~ *Source Unknown*

"Love doesn't make the world go around. Love is what makes the ride worthwhile."
~*Franklin P. Jones*

"You cannot be lonely if you like the person you're alone with."
~*Wayne Dyer*

"If others' love is not given voluntarily do not try to purchase it for purchased love often spoils quickly."
~*Andres Lara*

"Men always want to be a woman's first love. Women like to be a man's last romance."
~*Oscar Wilde*

"A bell isn't a bell 'till it's rung,
A song isn't a song 'till it's sung,
Love isn't love 'till it's given away."
~*Author Unknown*

Determination

66

The difference between possible and impossible lies in determination.

Determination is that, within you, which knows specifically what you want and refuses to accept anything else. That which has you get up no matter how many times you get knocked down. That which has you move forward in spite of how hopeless you feel.

Keep in mind that there is no obstacle, no destiny, and no fate that can ever stop someone who's determined to triumph.

"What this power is I cannot say; all I know is that it exists and it becomes available only when you get into that state of mind in which you know exactly what you want and are fully determined not to quit until you get it."   *~Alexander Graham Bell*

Commitment

Walt Disney was turned down 302 times before he got financing for his dream of creating the "Happiest Place on Earth". Today, due to his persistence and determination millions of people have shared 'the joy of Disney'. Colonel Sanders spent two years driving across the United States looking for restaurants to buy his chicken recipe. He was turned down 1,009 times! How successful is Kentucky Fried Chicken today? All of this because of the power of persistence and determination. ~*Author Unknown*

"I believe life is constantly testing us for our level of commitment, and life's greatest rewards are reserved for those who demonstrate a never-ending commitment to act until they achieve."
~ *Anthony Robbins*

"Those who can drive themselves further once their efforts get painful, are those who will win."
~ *Roger Bannister*

"A determined soul will do more with a rusty monkey wrench than a loafer will accomplish with all the tools in a machine shop." ~*Source Unknown*

Notes

Notes

<u>Notes</u>

<u>*Notes*</u>

ORDER OTHER BOOKS & TAPES BY THE SAME AUTHOR

Fax orders: 775-263-2686

Telephone orders: Have your VISA, MasterCard or American Express card ready.
973-281-9082. Check author's web site for the most up to date number.

On-line orders: **Email:** EverydayMotivator@hotmail.com, **Web:** www.TheCubanGuy.com

Postal orders: Andres Lara, PO Box 43577, Upper Montclair, NJ 07043 USA
     ** **Note:** Make sure to check www.TheCubanGuy.com or call for our current address)

I understand that I may return any book or tape in saleable condition for a full refund—
for any reason, no questions asked.

Please send the following books and tapes:

	Qty 1	Qty 500	Qty 100
Qty_____ Inspire The Sleeping Giant Within (book)	$ 19.95	$10	$7
Qty_____ How To Stay Motivated During Difficult Times (book)	$ 19.95	$10	$7
Qty_____ How To Move Forward When You Want To Quit (4 CD's)	$ 59.95	$20	$14
Qty_____ How To Rekindle The Fire In Your Relationship (book)	$ 19.95	$10	$7

Other:_____

Company name:_____

Address:_____

City:_____State:_____Zip_____

Telephone:_____Fax:_____

Email:_____

Shipping: $4.00 for first book, $1.97 for each additional book.
Get free shipping for large quantities (10 or more)

Payment: Check_____ Credit Card:_____ (circle on) Visa: MasterCard: Amex:

Total including shipping and sales tax: _____

Card Member: _____Exp. Date: _____

Name as it appears on card:_____

Signature: _____